Go for the Steak, Not the Sizzle

How to Find a Network Marketing Business that Really Works

Richard J. Warren

Go for the Steak, Not the Sizzle

How to Find a Network Marketing Business that Really Works

Richard J. Warren

Muddy Pig Press ◊ Las Vegas, Nevada

Richard J. Warren

Photo Credit: © Can Stock Photo Inc. / yekophotostudio

ISBN - 13: 978-0692504048

ISBN - 10: 0692504044

Printed in the United States of America

Muddy Pig Press ◊ Las Vegas, Nevada

In the long run, we shape our lives, and we shape ourselves. The process never ends until we die. And the choices we make are ultimately our own responsibility.

- Eleanor Roosevelt

Richard J. Warren

Table of Contents

Richard J. Warren

Author's Note

Many, many books have been written about network marketing, why in the world do we need another one? It's a question I asked myself many times over the years and always reached the conclusion that we don't. Another reason for my reluctance is the inevitable avalanche of sales pitches I would receive if I wrote such a book. Whenever I write an article in any way related to network marketing I'm inundated with people pitching the wonderful company they "discovered" and how it would be perfect for me. Mind you they know nothing about me nor do they care that I'm not at all interested in whatever they are selling. So then, why this book?

My first book, *A Rehabber's Tale*, explored the reality of fixing and flipping real estate for profit. My experience in the industry and success I achieved rehabbing real estate led a number of organizations to ask me to speak on the topic. At the conclusion one of these talks I was approached by a young woman who thanked me and told me she had attended a previous speaking engagement where I discussed how to evaluate a real estate deal and its profit potential. As we were talking she started to cry. She explained that the simple evaluation techniques I discussed prevented her and her husband from pulling the trigger on a deal that probably would have ruined them financially. The couple had been following the advice of a real estate agent who was most likely more interested in selling a piece of real estate than in their financial success. He probably knew very little about real estate investing though he professed otherwise. That was the moment I decided to write that first book and tell the truth about the rehabbing business.

Several years of writing the consumer column for *The Vegas Voice* newspaper led to my next book. My columns dealt with a myriad of consumer issues and many scams. I heard heart-breaking stories from readers about things that happened to them that often became the topics of my articles. Along the way I had the great fortune of meeting Elisabeth Daniels, then head of the State of Nevada's *Fight Fraud Taskforce*. In an effort to educate the public we co-authored *Scammers, Schemers and Dreamers - A Cautionary Tale for Consumers*. The book discusses how people get sucked in to get-rich-quick schemes and how to avoid becoming a victim.

So back to the question at hand, why this book? A number of people approached me and said that since I myself have achieved a degree of success in network marketing, much as I did in real estate rehabbing, I should write a book about the truth of that business as well. After all, it seems that everyone has either failed at an attempt to build a network marketing business or knows someone who has. Why do so many people fall for the hype and hope of network marketing only to be reduced to failure, and sometimes financial ruin, by the reality that is left when the hope and hype fades away? If they understood the reality of the industry perhaps they would have had a better chance at success. That's why I wrote this book.

While I don't profess to have all of the answers, nobody does, I do have a different way of looking at the business and have a good understanding of why people are not as successful as they could be. The book explores why people fail and encourages you to look at yourself to be sure that you aren't setting yourself up for disappointment. It may even convince you that network marketing is not for you at all.

The goal of this book is to give you the greatest possible chance for success if you do decide to try your hand at a home business. To be perfectly clear, it is not meant to be a rah-rah, you can do it, motivational pat on the back. There are plenty of books that do just that, and that is the purpose of most of those offerings. The book is also not intended to promote or indict any particular company or business. In fact, no specific companies will be mentioned in the book at all.

In the interest of simplicity, the phrase *network marketing* will be used to refer to a number of different types of companies. Many people use the phrase MLM or multi-level marketing to refer to these businesses, but that isn't correct. While all MLMs are network marketing companies, not all network marketing companies are MLMs, much like all Kleenex are tissues but not all tissues are Kleenex. Multi-level marketing is one business model used by network marketing companies but there are others as well.

I will also use the term *marketing executive* to describe those trying to build a network marketing business. Many companies use the term *distributor* to describe their sales force but not all companies do and many clearly do not have distributors at all. Marketing executive seems to be an apt description of people who are attempting to build a network marketing business. Feel free to insert whatever term you prefer.

Most importantly, this book is not intended to be a sales pitch. Many, if not most, books on network marketing are nothing more than sales pitches for the author and his or her company or opportunity. So read on with the assurance that this book is here to help.

Richard J. Warren

Chapter One

Introduction

Perhaps you've seen the commercials that say "work from home using your computer and earn thousands!" or "I made so much working from home that I bought a new house!" If you are paying attention you'll see all kinds of advertisements telling you that you can make $3,000, $5,000, $10,000 or more per month working from home. The truth is that those television ads are placed by lead generating companies that entice people to call only to sell the "hot leads" to network marketers. Many print and online ads are placed by network marketers hoping to get you to call so that they can tell you how to make those thousands every month even though they have probably never done so themselves.

How realistic are those ads? The short answer is not very realistic at all. The vast majority of people who venture into some network marketing opportunity will fail in short order. There are a lot of statistics that are bandied about, a common one is that 95% of all those who embark upon a network marketing business will fail. That particular statistic may be misleading in that it includes those who signed up as distributors or marketing executives in order to get better pricing on their own purchases but never intended to pursue it as a business. No matter how you dissect the statistics we are still dealing with a very, very large number.

Does that mean that if you were to start a network marketing business that you are doomed to fail? The answer to that is a resounding no. There are a number of network marketers who are fabulously successful, but they are few and far between. How can you be one of the successful few rather than the majority who will fail? First, by not repeating the mistakes of those who didn't do well, and second emulating the actions of those who did succeed.

My background as a *Certified Financial Planner* exposed me to a number of different businesses and I worked with many different business owners during my fifteen years in the financial services industry. Some of these entrepreneurs were extremely successful, others were barely hanging on, and the majority were somewhere in between. However, none of the ones I worked with had earned their living, let alone their fortune, through network marketing.

What I did come to find was that my profession caused me to have a bulls-eye placed squarely on my back. It seems that network marketers were told that they should talk to everyone who comes within three feet of them, but especially accountants, insurance agents, financial planners and others who were well connected. Over the years I was approached by so many people from almost every company in existence. My response to these individuals was that they should come back after they had been in business for more than one full tax year and have their IRS form 1099 in hand and then we could talk about it. It was a safe way of dealing with these unwanted approaches. None of them ever returned since most had left their new opportunity in short order or were too embarrassed to show how little they had actually earned.

I had also developed an enormous distaste for the way network marketers presented themselves. It seemed that for many of them it had become their life's mission to pester and annoy everyone that they came in contact with in an effort to advance their business. These are the people who walk into a room only to have everyone scatter just so that they didn't have to talk to them. If building a network marketing business meant that you needed to become a pariah in the community, then I wanted no part of it. There is a running joke in the home-based business community that you will soon become an exclusive member of the NFL club – *No Friends Left* – because you will have alienated anyone that you ever knew. This was a club that I had no intention of ever joining.

So how did I come to be involved in network marketing despite my strong negative feelings about the industry? Many psychiatrists believe that everything that has gone wrong in your life is somehow your mother's fault. That is certainly true in my case. While my mother never approached me about any business opportunity, she was certainly the catalyst that led me to network marketing.

The story began in the summer of 1995. At that time my mother had been working for the local county government in a job that she thoroughly enjoyed. While she was approaching retirement age, it was not something that she was thinking about. That changed suddenly when the county she worked for offered early retirement incentives for those who were close to retirement eligibility. The idea behind the incentives was to entice long-tenured employees to retire in order to save the county a substantial amount of money. While she didn't want to leave her job, the incentives were something that my mother had to consider.

Both my older and younger sisters were Certified Public Accountants and partners in a local accounting firm. When they reviewed my mother's incentive package they concluded that she had no choice but to accept the deal. Had she rejected the offer and waited to retire at a future date she would have had a lower pension and benefit package than the one being offered. There was one big problem with this scenario; she would not have enough money to live on. Based on her current budget, she would be left with a shortfall of about $500 per month. This meant that she would need to find a part-time job in retirement. The thought of my mother being one of those retirees working in a fast-food restaurant was not something that had any appeal to me or my sisters.

There are those who say that there are no coincidences in life, everything happens for a reason. That would seem to be the case here as well. I was on vacation that summer of 1995 when I received a call from my older sister. She told me that she had found a solution to my mother's dilemma and we needed to talk as soon as I returned home. She indicated that it was some sort of business opportunity and that I needed to see it. I made an assumption about what it was and wanted no part of it and did not bother call her when I got back home.

My sister had been helping someone evaluate a number of home-based businesses. It was a woman with five young children who needed to earn some extra money while being able to stay home with her kids. She also happened to be the wife of one of my sister's better clients so she, of course, accepted the assignment. In evaluating several different companies, my sister became familiar with a number of different product lines, compensation plans and risk factors involved. When the woman chose a company that had a very low start up cost and appeared to be risk free, my sister started thinking of our mother.

Ultimately my sister would not be ignored and I eventually sat down with her and we looked at the opportunity from my mother's perspective. Since she was my older sister, I remembered everything that she had ever done as I was growing up and thought of her as somewhat flaky (she really isn't) but I had also come to highly respect her business aptitude and judgment. So I did listen to what she had to say and came to realize, as she did, that there was no chance of my mother being hurt financially in this opportunity. As I saw it, the biggest risk was that she wouldn't be successful, just like most other people.

My sister and I created a plan that had each of us joining this company and then we went to work. We decided that we would go all-out for six months and then reevaluate everything. At the end of that time frame my mother was earning several hundred dollars a month and things had actually worked as we hoped they would, if not better. The by-product of this effort was that my sister and I were also earning several hundred dollars a month.

Fast-forward to today and my mother earns thousands of dollars a year and my sister and I earn substantially more – and we've been doing so for more than twenty years. None of us had ever been involved in any type of network marketing before. So how did we come to be among the few who achieved success rather than the majority who failed? By treating it the same way we did our primary businesses and not duplicating the mistakes that most people make when starting a business or choosing a company.

When I first joined the company I attended training meetings and devoured the available training material. While network marketing is often called a business of duplication, what we were being told seemed to be a duplication of the things that caused the majority of people to fail. It was the typical "make a list of everyone that you know," "speak to everyone that you come in contact with," "call to set appointments but don't tell people why they need to meet with you." This mindset was exactly what I found so abhorrent about the network marketing industry I refused to go along with it. If this is what I had to do, then I did not want to be in the business. I was told that I wasn't a team player, wasn't "coachable" and would never be successful I later learned that those telling people to do this had been with major MLM companies and were merely parroting what had been taught to them. It was not the company philosophy.

What I did do was treat this like a business I had invested tens of thousands of dollars to start. If I had opened up a brick and mortar retail establishment I wouldn't rely on friends and family for my success. Of course, if I did have a good business I would hope that they would support me, but I wouldn't expect them to feel obligated to do so. Yet network marketers are told to chase their friends and family and if their friends won't join then they aren't really your friends. Absolutely ridiculous!

There is another reality that you need to face as well, this business may not be right for you. Blasphemy, you say? How could that be? Isn't network marketing something that anyone can do? Well, yes and no. Theoretically anyone can do it, but not everyone is cut out to be successful in a network marketing venture. There are a number of reasons for this and we will examine them as we go along. We will also discuss how to evaluate companies, their products and compensation plan to separate the very few that are worthwhile from the vast majority that are not.

A note of caution: It is of the utmost importance to remain as objective as possible when evaluating an opportunity. If you are wearing rose-colored glasses when examining a company you will find the answers you *want* to find rather than the correct ones. That is called "confirmation bias" where you accept information that fits with your preconceived beliefs and disregard information that conflicts with them. A good example of this involves an article I wrote for a newspaper several years ago. The article was a cautionary piece warning consumers about home-business scams and listed ten evaluation points to consider if you were thinking about joining a network marketing company. Shortly after it appeared in print I received an email from a reader telling me had "discovered" a company that was exactly what I was looking for and met all my requirements. My article made it clear that I wasn't "looking" for anything but the reader must have missed that. The opportunity he was pitching failed miserably on eight of the ten evaluation points and the only people who had even a remote chance of making money were the people who started the company but even that was doubtful. The reader was obviously blinded by the hype the company was using to lure people in. That company has since gone out of business.

It is my hope that you will use this book as intended and first determine if a network marketing business is really for you at all. If so, evaluate opportunities with your eyes wide open and choose the company you partner with very carefully. Lastly do the business the right way and avoid repeating the mistakes that most people make.

Chapter Two

Real Promise or False Hope?

Why are so many lured into network marketing and other home-based income opportunities? For most it is the desire for a better tomorrow. Looking at the reality of their present station in life so many people are left searching for more. Perhaps the hopes and dreams of their current career path have been beaten down by the sledgehammer of reality. Maybe "Plan A" isn't working out and they are searching for a "Plan B." They could be trapped by circumstance and network marketing seems to offer a way out. But can the promise become reality?

So what is network marketing? Think of it in a reverse of the term – marketing to a network. The dictionary definition of a network in this context is: *an association of individuals having a common interest, formed to provide mutual assistance, helpful information, or the like* [**Dictionary.com**]. It is using people you know to help market your business. It does not necessarily mean targeting your contacts to sell to, but rather to have them help you grow your business through their contacts. Many business people rely on networking as a way of getting the word out about their business. The people in your immediate circle of contacts may not need or want what you can provide but they may know someone who does. Some would call that referral marketing in that you are referred to someone who needs your product or service.

Network marketing began almost a century ago as a way for companies to move product at relatively little cost to them. Independent distributors seeking to make extra money would purchase an inventory of products at wholesale prices with the intention of selling them to consumers at retail and pocketing the markup. For some it was a way to earn extra income, but for others it only made things worse when they accumulated an inventory of products they were not able to resell. A tongue-in-cheek term in network marketing is to become "garage qualified," that is when you have so much product inventory in your garage that it is no longer possible to park your car there.

The failure rate of distributors was extremely high yet people still flocked to these so-called opportunities. The companies themselves were profitable even though so much of their products wound up in the basements, garages and storerooms of their distributors without being sold. As these companies flourished other companies joined the industry. Some of the new companies merely copied the formula of the more established companies while others sought to improve on the business model.

Initially the companies were primarily moving goods through a distributor network but that, too, evolved. Due to improvements in technology and shipping many companies no longer required that product inventory be held for resale, items could be shipped directly to the end consumer without having to pass through a distributor chain. This resulted in network marketers becoming more of a marketing executive for a company rather than a distributor. It also lowered the cost of entry into many of these companies since a purchase of inventory was not always necessary.

There was another very real effect that all of these amateur entrepreneurs had on the network marketing marketplace. It caused a stigma to be attached to the industry and anyone involved in it. A good number of people do not respect network marketing as a "real business" and tend to look down on anyone who attempts to make their living from it. Every year thousands of people try their hand at a traditional entrepreneurial business, often investing their life savings and more, only to fail in a very short time. This attempt is usually respected even though it was unsuccessful. Yet if that same person starts a network marketing business they are stigmatized as "one of those people" doing "one of those pyramid things." What most of those critics fail to realize that just about every business is structured as a pyramid with the owner or CEO at the top followed by senior management and then the rank and file workforce. They call it a pyramid because of the pay plan but that is how most sales organizations are set up. Indeed, a pyramid is one of the most efficient structures in the universe. (This is not to be confused with illegal pyramid schemes or "Ponzi" schemes where money is passed from one person to the next with no exchange of value. These scams do exist and are often disguised as legitimate businesses.)

Today there are so many new network marketing companies yet their failure rate is almost as high as that of marketing executives. Some of these firms have something valuable to offer while others were created merely as a way to move money legally. The jungle that is capitalism is truly an arena where survival of the fittest is the rule, not the exception. The companies that are weak or do not have a competitive edge will fail in short order. Unfortunately when these companies fail they take their marketing executives down with them.

There is an old restaurant expression that says "you sell the sizzle, not the steak." The meaning is that you sell the emotional experience of the steak as opposed to the steak itself. You make the sale by connecting to the customer's emotions, not by using logic. Many of the network marketing companies sell exactly that way, by appealing to the emotional idea of what it would be like to be financially free. So many people buy into that idea without investigating whether the company that they are looking at, or any opportunity for that matter, is right for them.

All too often when people do investigate a company they often succumb to confirmation bias and find exactly what they want to believe. If they are predisposed to finding the positive they will tend to overlook the negative. If they are looking for an excuse to dismiss an opportunity they will find plenty of reasons to do so. Everyone has an opinion and the internet provides an easy forum to express it. If you try a simple internet search of any company, good or bad, people involved with the opportunity will tout how wonderful it is while others who want you to do something else (their opportunity) will bash it.

So how do you get past all of this clutter and get a true sense of whether a business opportunity is right for you? Look at the facts and ignore the hype. It's not easy to do but it is essential. What follows is a description of myths about network marketing, various types of businesses and a method of looking at the facts. Keep in mind that even a well-designed and well-run business may not be right for you as an individual. That's something that only you can determine.

Richard J. Warren

Chapter Three

Misconceptions, Myths & Lies

One of the reasons that many people have a distaste for network marketing is because of the lies they are told. Have you ever seen or heard a pitch that says "just sign up, it'll build itself" or "it's a ground-floor opportunity", or the classic – "you won't have to do any work." If it will build itself, or you don't have to do any work, who will? Network marketing is a business and it requires work, there is no free lunch.

Why would people expect that they can just sign up for something and the money will roll in? It certainly doesn't happen anywhere else in life. What you have are people who *want* to believe it's possible and others who will say anything to get prospects to enroll in their program. Those who have been told this and buy into that belief will pass it on to others. While there are some compensation plans that allow a very small amount of money to be passed to customers and marketing executives who haven't done much to deserve it, it is not possible to earn anything of significance without effort. Think about it from a business perspective, why would a company allow a large amount of money to be passed to someone who hasn't done anything to earn it? The short answer is that they wouldn't. If you are looking for a venture that doesn't require work on your part you may as well spend your time searching for unicorns.

Ground-Floor Opportunity

One of the great myths is that you have to "get in early" or find a "ground-floor opportunity." In any industry the vast majority of start-up businesses will fail early on. This truth has been demonstrated over and over again. Yet the myth is perpetuated by any new company that enters the network marketing industry. The theory is that there is great reward for those who take the risk of starting and succeeding in a new venture. This would be true if you were the one starting the company but not if you were joining as a marketing executive.

To attract new marketing executives on a long-term basis a company needs to have a product or service that people want and a compensation plan that is fair and balanced. The notion that it is somehow skewed to those who came first does not make any sense. If the deal for newcomers was significantly worse than for those who came first the company would have a hard time attracting new people as it got older. The idea that you benefit by having all of those who came later in your down-line doesn't wash either, no company can pay to infinity and stay in business.

A company with a proven track record can give you a better idea of what you can realistically expect to earn. An established company should also have a better history of stability. That's not to say that a company that's been around for a while can't fail, they certainly can and do. It's just that the odds are better for an established company to survive. You have people joining established companies everyday and experiencing success, the idea that you can't is ridiculous.

That doesn't mean that you shouldn't consider a start-up. Perhaps they have a new, cutting-edge product or concept to bring to the marketplace. Fortunes have been made by those talking a risk on a new venture but that is the exception rather than the rule. It's just the notion that getting in early on the ground floor is the only way that you can make money that doesn't hold water.

Saturation

Another myth is that a market is saturated. The 2010 Census determined that the population of the United States was 308,745,538. In 1970 it was 203,235,998 (official U.S. Census Bureau statistics). That's a whole lot of new customers, more than *105 million* of them. Even the largest corporations in the country continually expect to expand, why would a market for a network marketing company be saturated? How many customers do you need to be successful? They are certainly out there.

An issue of greater concern may be that the company that you are with, or considering joining, is unable to handle future growth. They may not have the capacity or ability to expand or innovate but that is a much different issue than saturation. If a company is not in a position to grow or expand you probably should be looking elsewhere anyway.

An issue that is real and may be disguised as saturation is one called *burn rate*. This is where companies have recruited so many hopeful marketing executives who failed and lost money doing so that the company developed a bad reputation. They have burned through so many people that they can't attract enough new ones. Some of these companies have tried to counter this reputation by changing their name or merging with or acquiring other companies and operating under that identity. Other companies have taken the much better step of changing their business model and practices in an effort to rehabilitate their reputation.

A better statistic to use would be penetration rate rather than saturation rate. How much has a company penetrated into a given market? The inverse of that number shows how much potential is left. It is not uncommon for a network marketing company to have only reached 1 or 2% of a given market. That leaves 98% or more left to be tapped. That is a tremendous opportunity for any company with a good product or service.

Walk-Away Income

A common misconception is that you can develop a "walk-away" income. What that essentially means is that you can build a business to the size that you desire and then walk away but have the money continue. The idea is that you are building a residual income that doesn't go away. That is wrong on a couple of different levels.

First there is the issue of attrition. Any business, no matter how good it is, will lose customers over time. Some industries have a high attrition, or turnover, rate while others may have a very low rate. Nevertheless there is a rate of attrition in every business and those customers need to be replaced to maintain the business at its present level. It doesn't matter if the business is a hardware store, pizza parlor or network marketing business, it will lose customers. People move, they die or they simply choose to do business elsewhere.

Another industry that heavily promotes the benefit of developing residual income is insurance. An agent writes policies and receives a residual commission each time that the policy is renewed and can, in time, become a substantial amount of money. But those policies still require service on occasion. If an agent retires or leaves the business he may continue to receive that residual but it will diminish over time. Some of the former clients will switch their business to other agents, other policies may lapse for various reasons and clients will die. The effect is that the residual will decline as time passes if new business isn't added.

You may say that others in your business will continue to bring in new customers, and that may very well be true to some extent. But what happens when they want to walk away? Sooner or later attrition will be a factor. That doesn't mean that you will not be able to scale back at some point, but you can't expect to walk away and maintain the status quo without effort.

Hopefully you will find yourself in a situation where you have built a substantial business. That usually means that you have built a strong team of people who look to you for leadership and support. Are you just going to walk away from them? What kind of example does that set for your team? What if your entire business decided to walk away at the same time?

You're Not Selling

Stop me if you've heard this one, "you're not selling, you're telling." Guess what? You're selling! When people think of salespeople they have the image of a used car salesman in a shiny suit selling an old clunker as a creampuff that was only driven by a little old lady on Sundays. They think that you have to lie and cheat in order to sell. The reality is that we are selling all the time. We may not be selling a particular item, perhaps we are simply selling our spouse on which restaurant to eat at. But it is selling. The best salesperson in the world is a toddler trying to convince you that it's a good idea for him or her to have a cookie before dinner.

What is selling? It is simply stating a position in regard to a particular item. Perhaps you are trying to convince someone about a political idea or which team is going to win the big game that day, it's all selling. Telling someone about your company or product is selling, and that isn't a bad thing. Twisting the truth or making false promises to get someone to buy something they do not need or want isn't selling, it's scamming.

People really shouldn't have a negative attitude about selling. Selling is informing a potential buyer about the features and benefits of something so that they can make an informed decision as to whether or not they should buy. If you cannot accept that selling is necessary and that it isn't evil, immoral or improper, then perhaps network marketing isn't right for you.

Some may think that because a prospect raises an objection that you need to pressure or convince them against their wishes. That just isn't so. There are two main reasons that people raise objections, one is that simply need more information in order to make a decision. The other one is a little more difficult to recognize, they raise objections because they don't want to tell you "no." Objections are a part of the sales process and are not necessarily a bad thing.

Make a List of Everyone You Know

One of the greatest misconceptions about network marketing is that you have to chase your family and friends in order to be successful. When people join a network marketing company one of the first things that they are told is to make a list of everyone that they even remotely know. That list should contain every friend, relative, business associate, and anyone who ever came within three feet of them from the day they were born. Then they are supposed to contact them immediately in order to tell them about this amazing opportunity they just discovered. Hogwash.

This alone is one of the reasons that many people despise network marketing and why the industry has such a stigma attached to it. This one simple instruction conjures up images of people hounding everyone that they come in contact with until they have alienated everyone that they have ever known. Try to recall the last time you were at some event or party, were you approached by a dentist, doctor, auto mechanic, or local merchant who tried to sell you on their service. Has that ever happened? Probably not but you can surely recall the last time that someone approached you about the latest network marketing opportunity. If you want to be treated with the respect that other professionals receive then act like a professional.

While I do agree that you need to create such a list, it is not done for the purpose of hounding these people from the moment you join a network marketing company. You create a list is to see if there is anyone that you absolutely should be contacting immediately, but not to call them all the moment you join. The professional way is to have people approach you. You do this by making it known that you are in a particular business and let those who are curious and want to know more ask you. As you market yourself and word gets out you will wind up talking to all of those on your list at some point anyway. Being a nuisance simply alienates people.

There are many network marketers who would absolutely disagree with this idea. They are generally the ones who are training their people to do the very things that give the industry a bad name. They treat it strictly as a numbers game; the more people that you approach the more you will ultimately sign up. But how many people will you alienate and how many bridges will you burn before you have a real understanding of your business?

It Won't Work Here

One of the big lies is one that people tell themselves. They convince themselves that it is impossible to build a business where they live. They are certain that it will work, but only somewhere else. They say that if they were in such and such a place they would be able to build a business easily. They are only justifying their own inability to meet with success. It is just as hard to build a business in the next town, city or state as it is where they live.

It is true that every part of the country is different in some way, that each has its own personality and style. While the nuances of building a business may be different due to these local styles, it is not any easier or harder somewhere else. You just need to adapt to the location you are in, especially if you move from one area to another. The population density may be a factor in terms of the number of prospects in any given area, but it will also be a factor in the amount of competition that you will face. It all evens out in the end. If you find yourself using the "it won't work here" excuse, pause and take a deep breath. Location does not make it harder or easier, it just makes it different. If it will work in one place it will certainly work in another.

Fake It Till You Make It

One of the worst, and often most harmful, lies is that you should fake it until you make it. There was a time when this theme was touted by a lot of companies and their representatives. The idea was that you should spend money in order to appear successful, even if you weren't. A lot of people would do just that and buy fancy cars, expensive suits, a fancy watch, and other status symbols. It was supposed to fool people into thinking that you were a huge success and they could be to if they joined you and the company you represent. Unfortunately it usually doesn't work that way. Most people will see through the deception pretty quickly and your credibility may be damaged beyond repair. People who fake it only to fail in their business venture wind up with cars, clothes and other trappings of success that they can't afford. This charade is another reason that network marketing has a stigma attached to it.

If you have a good opportunity and are presenting it to a person with a reasonable amount of intelligence it isn't necessary to fake it. There is nothing wrong with saying that you are just getting your business started. Your prospect needs to determine if the opportunity is something that would be right for them. If they sense that you are faking it, and they probably will, then they may feel that this is the way that the business is supposed to be done and conclude that they don't want any part of it. Honesty will give you a much better shot at success than deception ever will.

A lot of marketing executives are embarrassed by the fact that they aren't making a lot of money. They may only be making a few hundred dollars each month and think that this won't entice anyone to join them. If only they were making $10,000 or more per month it would be easy – wrong! A lot of people will find a big check intimidating because they feel that they could never earn that or that it would be too much work.

Others see that big check and think that they can earn that quickly with very little effort. Many people can relate to a smaller check much easier than a big one. Just present the opportunity in an honest and open manner and everyone will be much better off, especially you.

Summary

These are just a few of the myths, lies and misconceptions that you will come across, there are many others. In dealing with the former Soviet Union on the issue of arms control, Ronald Reagan had this to say: "Trust, but verify." What that essentially means is that you should take nothing at face value. Even if you hear it from a trusted source you should verify the accuracy of the information. You need to be careful not to buy into the falsehoods that seem to be accepted as facts by a great number of people.

Richard J. Warren

Chapter Four

Reasons for Failure

There are so many reasons why people fail in business. The Bureau of Labor Statistics estimates that approximately one quarter of businesses fail in their first year of operation, more than half fail within five years and fewer than 25% will survive for ten years. Some reasons are obvious, such as lack of sufficient capital, while others may be more subtle. Network marketing is a business like any other and a certain amount of failure is to be expected. However, network marketing is unique in that many people who attempt it would never try their hand at a more traditional business. The reason so many people attempt one is because the cost of entry is very low compared to starting a traditional businesses, specialized knowledge is not generally required, and and it is possible to keep your present job while you establish your network marketing organization.

This ease of starting up can be a blessing as well as a curse. If you were to invest $250,000 of your life savings in a business venture you would certainly give it a solid effort and devote 100% of your energy to make it successful. How many people would give that same time, energy and commitment to a business that only cost them $250 to start? The answer to that is not many, most will quit as soon as it becomes even a little bit difficult. They bought the sizzle of life changing income but lost interest when the steak turned out to be a little too tough for their liking.

Let's take a closer look at some of the major reasons for failure.

Not Motivated

Complaining about your station in life seems to be the national pastime. We hear people moaning and groaning about their job, not having enough money or time and so on. Yet how many people take even the smallest steps to do anything about it? Not very many of them. As much as people hate wherever it is they may be in life, they fear change even more. It is much easier to accept the status quo than it is to take the action necessary to change it.

People love to talk about all of the things they are going to do. Noted motivational speaker, Zig Ziglar, calls this *Someday Isle*. Someday I'll do this; someday I'll do that, but someday never seems to arrive. We all know people who are all talk and no action; they'll say things like "I'm so motivated" but their actions say otherwise. Maybe you're one of those people. If so, it's not too late to change.

Realistically speaking, most people are not motivated to change. Change means upsetting their routine and we are all creatures of habit to some extent. Change also means that we may have to give up something we care about. Perhaps we can't play as much golf or watch our favorite TV show. Change usually involves sacrifice that few people are willing to make.

We hear people talk about motivating their team or doing things in the name of motivating someone. However, this is something that is impossible to do. You cannot motivate someone, period, case closed. Motivation comes from within, it's either there or it isn't.

Not Committed

Mike Krzyzewski, otherwise known as Coach K, of the Duke University Blue Devils had this to say about commitment:

Make a distinction between interest and commitment. When you are interested in something you do it only when it is convenient. When you are committed you do it all the time, no matter what.

Who wouldn't be interested in having a better life, or having more money along with actually having the time to enjoy it? The sad thing is that while just about anyone can improve their life, very few are willing to make the commitment to do so. Commitment requires change and as noted earlier, change is scary to most people. Remember the old adage: If you keep doing what you've always done you will keep getting what you've always gotten.

On the surface, motivation and commitment may seem to be the same thing. However they are, indeed, different. Commitment is long-term and keeps you driving towards your ultimate goal while motivation is what keeps you going on a daily basis. They certainly have a strong relationship with each other and it is your long-term commitment that fuels your motivation.

Unrealistic Expectations

Do you know someone who is a real dreamer? That person who seems to have sky-high expectations? You will find that a lot in network marketing. Imagine someone who has never achieved any significant level of success or earned a great deal of money, this same person joins a network marketing company and suddenly expects to be making $500,000 per year. Of course that doesn't happen and they will generally quit within a very short period of time while blaming everything and everyone but themselves for their failure. That's not to say that someone making $50,000 annually can't go on to earn $500,000 per year in network marketing. It can and does happen, but it isn't easy and it doesn't happen overnight. Think back to any job that you ever had, did you instantly know everything that you needed to? No, of course not, there is a learning curve involved in even the simplest of jobs and network marketing is no different.

Network marketing offers just about anyone chance for success. That doesn't mean that there is no work involved or learning required. Just as riding a bicycle is usually learned by using training wheels, network marketing is learned in small steps. Certain life experience is helpful and can accelerate that learning, but there is no magic bullet. Just about every network marketing company has many stories of people who joined and seemed to achieve instant success. However you will usually find that these overnight sensations had been involved with some other company where they cut their teeth and gained the experience necessary to succeed.

Ego Involved

Who doesn't know someone who always seems to be worried about what other people think? They are so concerned about their image and how others perceive them. They buy in to the stigma that is often associated with those who engage in network marketing. They act as if it is beneath them and they could never be "one of those people." But are the people whose approval they are seeking going to pay their bills? Of course not.

Fortunately most people who feel network marketing is beneath them will never join in the first place.

If you can't check your ego at the door you will have a very hard time in this business. You have to put up with a lot of negativity and deal with people who think that what you do isn't a legitimate business. Anyone who is successful has also experienced a significant amount of rejection, the more successful that someone is the more times they have heard the word "no." If that is something that your ego can't deal with you may be better off trying your hand at something other than network marketing.

Confidence

A big reason for failure in many areas of life is a lack of confidence in one's ability. Often the difference between someone who succeeds and another who doesn't is simply a matter of belief. Henry Ford once said: "if you think you can, or if you think you can't, you're right." Someone who doesn't have confidence in their ability tends to exhibit that subliminally to those that they interact with. People will subconsciously pick up on the signals that you are sending out. A confident person has a posture that says that they believe in what they're saying and their prospect will pick up on that belief. All things being equal, confident people will usually experience much more success than those who don't believe in themselves.

There are many reasons why someone does not feel confident. Sometimes it simply stems from a lack of knowledge or familiarity about their company or product. That is remedied quite simply with experience or knowledge acquired over time. More often this lack of confidence comes from insecurities that the person has. These insecurities develop over a lifetime and aren't as easy to correct. It can be something that has been ingrained from an early age and accumulated over a long period of time.

So how do you correct that? If there was an easy answer psychologists everywhere would be looking for a new line of work. That doesn't mean it can't be done. We all have self-limiting beliefs and insecurities that keep us from being the best that we can be. Those who are able to overcome them can be hugely successful. Unfortunately most people allow these beliefs to hold them back. That is why such a small percentage of people ever reach the top of any profession.

Experiencing success, however small, will help people build that internal belief in themselves. Success leads to confidence which leads to more success, which leads to more confidence, which leads to more success, and so on. Unfortunately, failure also works this way. Failure can erode confidence which leads to more failure. It can be a difficult cycle to break. If you have a problem with confidence, there any dozens of self-help books and programs that can assists you in improving your situation.

Fear of Rejection

Many people have a difficult time handling rejection. It is a very close cousin to a lack of confidence. Every time you are rejected, especially by someone that you know, your confidence suffers. The word "no" has been ingrained in us as bad from the time we were babies. We were told no so often that we ultimately fear it. However the primary difference between a network marketer who is successful and one who isn't is that the successful person has received many, many more rejections.

Rejection is very much a part of the business and there is no way around it. You are going to hear the word no, if you can't handle that then you should be looking for another type of business. While it isn't always easy to do so, we have to learn not to take rejection personally. It is not you that is being rejected but the opportunity that you are presenting. Yet some people take every rejection as a personal attack and some individuals find it so devastating that they can't continue in the business.

Having difficulty with rejection isn't unusual at all. Even those who make a living telemarketing and selling over the phone have trouble with this. Telemarketers probably experience more rejection than anyone and can develop what is known as "call reluctance." They become fearful of hearing the word no and will avoid making calls. Can you think of a time when you planned to make calls but conveniently found other really important things that needed to be done, like cleaning your desk or doing laundry?

Think of the waiter in the coffee shop who walks around offering coffee to each customer. Some say yes and others say no. The waiter isn't devastated when someone rejects his offer of coffee, he just moves on to the next customer. That is how you should think of your network marketing prospects, just customers in your coffee shop, if they don't want the coffee just go to the next prospect.

Negativity

Right up there with rejection is negativity, which is simply another form of rejection. Have you ever told someone of your plan to begin a network marketing business only to have them say "those things don't work" or something to that effect? If network marketing doesn't work why are there so many network marketing companies? Many of these companies have been in existence for decades, how would that be possible if "those things" didn't work?

What that usually means is that network marketing didn't work for them or someone that they know. Look at the person who is telling you this, how successful are they at whatever they do? It seems that many people have a fondness for putting things down. The problem is that many times these are people that we know well and we have a tendency to take what they say at face value even though they may not have any specific knowledge to back up what they say.

Negativity is something that you are going to face. It can be difficult to deal with, especially if that negativity comes from someone close to you, such as a spouse or family member. Negativity has caused a great many people to fail before they even got their business started. If you do not have the support of your spouse network marketing can be extremely difficult to succeed at. If you can't deal with the negativity that you are sure to encounter network marketing may not be right for you.

Not Coachable

Any company that has achieved some degree of success usually has systems in place and successful people to help guide others. They will generally have some type of presentation prepared that is designed to highlight the company, product line and business opportunity. It is meant to make the business easier, encourage duplication, and increase the chance of success for someone who joins the company. Yet there are always those who attempt to reinvent the wheel. They think that they know it all and they could do it better their way.

Professional athletes who may have achieved the highest levels of excellence in their respective sports still have coaches guiding them. The idea is to learn from those who have gone before you and to have them analyze your performance in search of areas that could be improved. People who resist the efforts of others to help them or who refuse to utilize the tools that their company provides are not considered *coachable* and have a diminished chance of success.

That is not to say that you should blindly follow every piece of advice given. One of the problems with network marketing is that so much of what is taught is wrong. While this may seem to be a contradiction, being coachable really means that you are willing to heed the advice of those that you respect. If you have a mentor who does the business the way that you would like to, then you should be open to being coached by that person.

If you are coachable you will take the advice that you respect and adapt it to suit your own personality and style. Watching the actions of those who do business the way you would like to, emulating their methods and incorporating into your own style is an excellent way to build a business. The person who is not coachable will not listen to anyone and will stubbornly insist on doing things his own way. This person has almost no chance of success.

Trying to Save the World

When someone finds something that they feel is an answer to all of their hopes dreams and prayers they automatically think of other people who are in the same situation. They figure that these people will see the opportunity and jump on it, just as they did. They create their contact list and start calling on all of the people they know that has a need for money. These wanna-be saviors are flabbergasted when they are rejected time and time again. They just don't understand what is wrong with these people, why can't they see it?

The problem doesn't lie with the people they are talking to, it lies with them. They find themselves on a mission to save people who have no desire to be saved. The sad truth is that people are where they are in life for a reason. The people they are trying to save do not want their help; they are comfortable where they are. What they are proposing to these people would require them to make changes that they have no desire to make.

It is a natural tendency to try to help people who have a need, but it usually doesn't work. Sure, you can get a lot of these people to sign up but very few of them will ever do anything with the opportunity. Instead of seeking out people with a need, they should be looking for people who are already successful at something else. People tend not to approach those who are already successful because they think that they don't "need" it. But you shouldn't be looking for those who need it but, rather, those who want it.

That's not to say that there aren't people with a need for money who wouldn't be successful. There are many people who have a deep burning desire for success but haven't found a vehicle that is right for them yet. Finding someone like that can be like striking oil. That is a difficult person to find but well worth the effort.

Keep in mind that water seeks its own level. Needy people have a tendency to always be needy. However, successful people are often open to additional ways to enhance their level of success. The problem is that all too often they aren't approached. It's like the beautiful girl who doesn't get invited to the prom because the guys all assume that someone else has already asked her.

Company Chosen

There are so many different types of companies to choose from and a company that is right for one person may be the absolute wrong for someone else. Everyone has a different personality and it is important to choose a company to work with that fits that person's personality type or they will have a difficult time. There are many stories of someone who starts with one company only to fail miserably who then signs on with a totally different company and ultimately meets with success. But for every person who failed with company A and found success with company B you can usually find someone who did just the opposite, failed with company B but did well with company A.

The fault didn't lie with the company but rather with the marketing executive, they simply chose the wrong company for them. There are some people who love to retail products while there are many others who would never achieve success with that type of company. Some people do well with a simple line of merchandise while others find excitement in cutting-edge products or the latest technology. Where some want a company that has a wide variety of offerings, still others prefer the simplicity of a company that has only one or a few products.

There are so many different types of companies, products, marketing plans and pay structures. Choosing the correct one for you will have a lot to do with how much success you experience. Unfortunately many people are introduced to a company by someone that they know and sign up based on that relationship. They don't do very much due diligence in order to determine if they are suited to that particular company's way of doing business. Still others will try and fail and blame the industry itself for their failure. There may well be a company that would have been right for them but after failing the first times they are never willing to give it another shot.

Junkies

There are an astonishing number of people that I like to refer to as *network marketing junkies*, or MLM junkies. These are the people who never met a company they didn't like and have joined them all, it seems, at one time or another. Every time you see them they are doing something different. If there is a hot new start-up they are there, if they meet someone who is doing well with an established company, they are jumping into that one next. The common thread that seems to run through all of these individuals is that they have not achieved a great deal of success with any of the companies that they've joined.

There is an old saying that states: A dog that chases two rabbits doesn't catch either one. Being successful at anything requires a commitment, representing more than one company makes it extremely difficult to do well in any of them. People will say that one company doesn't interfere with another, but it has to. To be successful you need to find a company and give it 100% of your attention and effort. If you don't, what kind of a message does it send to those you are working with or trying to recruit?

Another issue is that it quickly becomes clear that you aren't committed to what you are doing. How can you expect people to take you seriously if you don't take yourself or your business seriously? If you are trying to work with several different companies at the same time you should stop immediately. If you are jumping from company to company ask yourself "why?" Take a good hard look at what you are doing. Choose the one company that offers what you are seeking, if none of them do then you need to find a company that does. Make a commitment to that company and take a solemn vow that you will not join any other companies, no matter how tempting it may be.

Hobby or Business?

Is network marketing a hobby or a business? For some it's a hobby and they treat it as such, they don't want much out of it and if they make a few dollars, fine. For most it's a business, yet they still treat it like a hobby. They do it for a little while, then they don't, then they start again only to stop once more. If they don't take the business seriously, how can they ever expect to be successful? Like any business, in order to be successful you need to have a business plan with real goals and expectations. You need to have "store hours" when you are open to work your business and take the steps necessary for success. A hobby-like business will have hobby-like results.

Most people don't treat network marketing as a business for the simple reason that they have never run a business before. Unfortunately most of the training involves how to approach people, set appointments and make presentations. Very little attention is given to actually running a business and many people will fail for this reason.

Give Up Too Easily

A major reason why people aren't successful is that they give up too easily. Instead of learning from their mistakes and improving their business, they just quit. Many will stop as soon as things get a little difficult. Perhaps they have worked through their warm prospect list and don't know how to find new business (another reason for not relying on friends and family to build a business). In many cases they could have been successful if they had just kept going. These people are snatching defeat from the jaws of victory, quitting when on the verge of success. Many of them probably would have kept going if only they knew what to do next. Instead they quit in frustration.

Many successful network marketers achieved success simply because they kept going when others would have quit. There is definitely something to be said for perseverance. How often have you heard stories of people who persevered through difficult times only to achieve great things? Thomas Edison failed 1,000 times in his attempt to invent a light bulb. Rather than view it as a failure he stated, "The light bulb was an invention

---

with 1,000 steps." Experiencing failure before ultimately being successful happens in business, science, sports, and life in general, why would network marketing be any different?

Summary

While there are certainly dozens more reasons why people fail, these are the major ones. Which ones apply to you? Some certainly do. We are all human and to be successful at anything requires that we overcome the roadblocks we set up for ourselves. Are you willing to put forth the effort required to do so?

Chapter Five
The Dark Side of MLMs

Many of the home-based business opportunities available today are multilevel marketing (MLM) based so it is important to understand what an MLM is. Unfortunately many are more about moving money than marketing any real product. Simply put, a company that does not offer legitimate products that people really want and sell them at a reasonable price will not last. People may come in for the perceived financial opportunity, but without something of value to offer the consumer the expected money will not materialize. Fortunately these types of companies are not the only game in town but far too often they do seem to be the ones generating the most buzz.

Many people who do not understand the distinction tend to refer to all home based business as MLMs or multilevel marketing. While it may be convenient to throw all companies into one bucket and call it MLM, it is not correct.

The Federal Trade Commission (FTC) Bureau of Consumer Protection has this to say about MLMs: *In multilevel or network marketing, individuals sell products to the public – often by word of mouth and direct sales. Typically, distributors earn commissions, not only for their own sales, but also for sales made by the people they recruit.* [www.consumer.ftc.gov/articles/0065-multilevel-marketing]

The FTC goes on to provide a cautionary note: *Not all multilevel marketing plans are legitimate. If the money you make is based on your sales to the public, it may be a legitimate multilevel marketing plan. If the money you make is based on the number of people you recruit and your sales to them, it's not. It's a pyramid scheme. Pyramid schemes are illegal, and the vast majority of participants lose money.*

Many people erroneously believe that the term multilevel refers to the compensation structure and that marketing executives are paid on multiple levels. What multilevel actually refers to is that there are multiple levels of product distribution with people paying different prices based on their position, or "level," in the distribution chain. In terms of pay almost every company pays on multiple levels. Think of it like this: Owner > General Manager > Manager > Assistant Manager > Supervisors > Rank-and-file Employees. Sales organizations have a similar structure. MLM simply refers to the method of distribution.

Personally it's a source of amusement when I tell people I never have been, nor would I ever be, involved with a multilevel marketing company. That statement usually results in a confused look on the face of the person I'm speaking to and leads to the question "But aren't you with...?" They don't understand what an MLM is and that my company isn't one. For some that type of business is just fine but it doesn't suit me.

Multilevel marketing companies have been around for almost a century. It was viewed as a low-cost method of selling products because distribution cost and much of the risk was shifted from the manufacturer to an independent distributor. It has evolved over the years and many companies have adopted the method. The internet has allowed for exponential growth in the creation of MLM companies. Creating them is one thing, having them survive an entirely different matter. Many, if not most, of these MLM startups are little more than a flash in the pan. One company comes up with an idea and gets off to a fast start, others quickly copy the plan and start a competing business until the fad passes and they all die off. That is why a careful evaluation of any opportunity is key, you don't want to hop on a fad.

A Well-Earned Stigma

Anyone who operates a network marketing business is going to encounter the stigma associated with MLMs. The unfortunate part is that the majority of the population doesn't understand the differences and tosses every home-based business into the MLM bucket and thinks of it as "one of those things." This didn't just happen; it is the result of practices employed by all too many multilevel marketing companies. It is also the reason why I would never choose to do business with an MLM company. If you decide to take that route be sure you are aware of the pitfalls and go in with your eyes wide open.

As stated earlier the MLM model was pioneered by companies looking for an innovative way to move products. This was a low-cost method that allowed the company to partner with an independent sales force in a way that spread the risk but also shared the profits. On the surface this was a win-win proposition. So what went wrong?

There were a number of inherent flaws in the early MLM model. Distributors were recruited with the expectation that they would sell or "distribute" products to customers. This direct sales approach meant that the distributors needed inventory on hand. This often meant a large initial investment in products. There was also a monthly purchase requirement that was well in excess of what a distributor could use personally so any excess would be added to the product inventory. All too often these distributors had little, if any, sales experience and had a hard time moving the product. This meant a significant inventory backlog and a loss of perhaps thousands of dollars. It happened so often that it became known as being "garage qualified" when there was so much product in the garage the car would no longer fit.

These distributors were also expected to recruit others into the business and that was where expectations of significant income came from. When others were recruited the "sponsor," or person who recruited them, would earn commissions on whatever their recruits sold. This would become the distributor's downline. The recruitment of new distributors was usually where people would focus their attention, which of course meant they weren't selling any product themselves. The new distributor would have to purchase inventory which would result in a large commission for the recruiter. The practice of having to purchase so much inventory was known as front-loading and is one of the major reasons for people being harmed financially.

The way people are paid can also be an issue. The commission on product sales encouraged recruiters to front-load their new distributors but there were other problems down the road. If someone recruited a distributor that did well they were happy to earn commissions on that person's effort for a while. If that recruit did very well and their sales volume reached a certain level they would "break away" from their sponsor. Good for the distributor but bad for the person that recruited them. The recruiter's commission would drop drastically as a percentage of sales. The theory is that the recruiter would find and develop a new distributor and repeat the process. The reality is that few ever did so.

As the initial companies achieved success plenty of imitators followed. The motivation for many of these new companies was not using the model as a way to move product but simply as a vehicle to move money. Many fads came and went over the years. They would soar initially, be copied by others who wanted to capitalize on the hype and then they would fail, sometimes in spectacular fashion.

Many of the fads were in the nutritional field where it was easy to make claims based on some pseudo-science. These claims would be touted by a doctor who on more than one occasion purchased a fake degree or obtained one from a non-accredited school or diploma mill. The companies selling things such as shark cartilage, colloidal minerals, liquid vitamins, vitamins made from fruits and vegetables, super antioxidant juices, magic bracelets, and even chocolate. Most of the claims could easily be debunked if only people bothered to investigate, but of course they didn't. Had they checked they could have found that: tests showed that a bottle of antioxidant juice that cost $30 or more wasn't any better than the $4 bottle of brand name grape juice from the supermarket; that the super-chocolate wasn't any better than a bar of dark chocolate that was a fraction of the price; vitamins lose their efficacy in liquid form; sharks do get cancer and using a supplement based on their cartilage won't prevent it; yes it is recommended that people get 5-9 servings of fruits and vegetables every day but that's mostly because of the fiber needed, the process of manufacturing vitamins from fruits and vegetables removes all the fiber and therefore does not meet the daily requirement. And so it goes. Why don't people investigate? Money. They fall for the hype, sales pitch, and visions of dollars piling up in their bank account.

Another problem with MLMs, and indeed other networking businesses as well, are the compensation plans. Most are designed to concentrate money in the hands of the top people yet they are often touted as being "powerful" and a way for the little guy to make money. They are often gimmicky and camouflage the fact that it is very difficult to make any money at all. The breakaway model was described earlier but you should also watch out for plans that "pay to infinity" which is mathematically impossible. So-called cutting edge plans such as binary are depicted as revolutionary but they have significant flaws such as only paying on one portion of your business – the weaker one.

Many later version of MLMs are little more than pyramid schemes disguised as a legitimate business. The internet has allowed companies to create a website that offers some essentially worthless product with order fulfillment handled by a third party. The focus of the business and the compensation comes from recruiting, not from product sales. One of two things will happen here, the company will get shut down or they will fail when they run out of people to con.

The bottom line is that if you are serious about having a successful business for the long term it should be a solid company that offers something of real value to the consumer. The majority of the MLM companies do not fit that description. Fortunately there are different types of network marketing companies that do. The difficulty lies in sorting through the garbage to find that unicorn and that is the topic of the next chapter.

Chapter Six

Evaluating an Opportunity

Home-based business opportunities come in many different shapes, sizes, and styles. One that immediately comes to mind for most people is MLM or multi-level marketing companies. These generally have distributers selling products retail and trying to recruit others into the opportunity. Often these companies are selling products they do not manufacture themselves but try to make people think that they do. There are Party Plan companies, offering things such as candles, essential oils, food storage, and even lingerie and the representatives will have someone host a party in order to sell product and recruit other distributors. Some are companies are selling services, such as communications or travel and there are others selling insurance products and legal services. In addition there are manufacturers selling products directly to consumers using marketing executives to recruit customers and other marketing executives.

There is also a new breed that is little more than a vehicle to move money with any products simply an afterthought. Products are often provided by a third party and only used to avoid being labeled a Ponzi scheme. Companies that are skirting the boundaries of legality will often come up with the compensation plan first and then search for a product or service to sell. These companies are more about collecting fees for signing people up than about the sale of any real product and should be avoided. Be sure the company is offering something of real value to the consumer, if it is then proceed with the evaluation.

Before you even bother to delve into the company look at what you would have to do as a marketing executive. Are you comfortable with that type of selling? Does it fit in with your lifestyle? If the answer is "no" there is no need to go any further, but if you feel it may be a good fit then it is time to dig much deeper into the opportunity.

What follows is a list of ten evaluation points to consider. If it is truly a good opportunity there should be positive results for all ten. Mind you, only a very few companies will meet all ten but remember – you only need one, so why not one of the best? If you do choose to ignore or overlook one of the evaluation points you will be increasing your risk of failure. Ignore more than one and the failure risk increases exponentially so think hard before doing so. If the results of your investigation are acceptable to you then proceed with confidence but understand that success is by no means assured. Some of the information you need should be fairly easy to obtain while other facts may be more difficult to find and may require some detective work on your part. Be wary of your sources and consider if that particular source may have a vested interest in the results you find. The company itself may seem like a good source of information but remember, they are going to spin the information in a way that paints them in the most favorable light. Remember the Ronald Reagan quote – *"trust, but verify."*

Evaluation Points

1- Company Track Record, Management & Finances

This one is right at the top yet it is so often overlooked. People will join a company because a friend or relative asked them to, but they will do so without ever looking into the background of the company or examining its operation. It is important to know how long the company has been around and what its track record has been. It is common knowledge that a great number of companies will fail in the early years of their existence. A company that has been around for many years and weathered a number of market cycles, recessions, and such has a much higher likelihood of being around for the long term. The "ground floor" nonsense is usually what you hear from brand new companies touting some fad product that is the modern day magic elixir. Sure some of them may be good opportunities, but one with a proven track record of success is probably a better bet.

The management team will tell you a lot about a company. Have they been bouncing from one MLM (multi-level marketing company) to the next or do they have a strong business background in corporate America? It is not uncommon to find someone who started one company, milked it for all it was worth and then started a new venture and started doing it all over again. Those companies should be avoided. An internet search can usually yield quite a bit of information about a company and its executives. When doing those searches always be mindful of who is providing the information as they may have an agenda and are slanting the information in a way that fits their purpose.

Company finances are vitally important. Debt-free would be ideal though not that common. If company debt is manageable and cash flow is sufficient you are on the right track. If a company is struggling to pay its bills that is a huge red flag. Financial information is easy to obtain if the company is public (listed on a stock exchange). It will be more difficult to find in privately held entities. However, privately held companies have an advantage in that their primary concern is not their shareholder's profit.

1A - Regulatory / Legal Issues

This goes hand-in-hand with the company's track record. Is the company under investigation or have they been disciplined by regulators? What about the management team? Have they been in trouble with the current or previous companies? Following the regulatory trail will tell you a lot about a company and their practices. There have been many cases of people getting in trouble with one company, starting another and doing the same thing again. This is not something you should ignore.

As of the summer of 2015 one of the major MLM companies is under investigation by the Federal Trade Commission for operating an illegal pyramid scheme. The FTC is considering whether the company is less focused on the sale of products and instead pushing recruitment of marketing executives. This company's business model has been copied by many others and if the regulators take this one down many others could follow in domino fashion.

2- Product Line

This is another factor that people tend to gloss over but it is hugely important. Is it a product or service that people need? Is it one they want? If they want it but don't need it then it may be considered a luxury item and one they can do without if finances are tight. If it's one that is needed at all times the business would probably do better in a difficult economic time such as a recession.

Are the products real? That is, are the products something a consumer would purchase anyway or is there some extraordinary hype behind them? The over-hyped products tend to be nothing more than a fad and fads do not last. An example would be the antioxidant juices. So many companies were pushing these juices and making a number of extraordinary claims regarding their health benefits. It was a product people had never used before and was sold mostly on these sensational claims. Many of these companies rose rapidly only to crash and burn in a spectacular fashion. Because it was a product people had never used before it was easy for them to stop using it when they didn't experience the health benefits or, more likely, didn't make the money they anticipated.

Sometimes a product will have a temporary price advantage in the marketplace. A good example of this would be the long distance telephone service resellers. For a time they were able to significantly undercut the major phone companies and many of their marketing executives did very well. When long distance rates fell drastically that price advantage was gone and the companies collapsed. The businesses that people spent time and energy building were gone seemingly overnight.

The key question is: does the company offer a product(s) that people are already using? If not, why would they need or want to use it? Is that reason compelling enough that they would keep using it under any circumstance? The best chance for success would be offering a product that was necessary and simply requires a consumer to switch brands, not acquire new habits. Consumers tend to be creatures of habit but are extremely reluctant to change old ones or develop new ones.

3- Competitive Advantage / Timing

If the product is indeed something that people need and want why would they buy this particular brand as opposed to one that is already established? It is necessary to have a competitive advantage. Many companies have products that, while of good quality, don't have any advantage over others already established in the marketplace. Quite often they cost significantly more than the products they are trying to compete with. The only reason people buy them is because there is a perceived opportunity to earn money. When that money doesn't materialize in sufficient quantity they leave the program and stop buying the product. That's hardly a very good recipe for long-term success.

Are the products unique in some way? If they aren't very different from those that already exist in the marketplace the company would need to have a price advantage of some kind in order to survive. Trying to compete solely on price is difficult at best. If the price advantage should disappear the company may not be able to survive. The perfect example of this is again the long-distance telecommunications companies. When they had significantly lower rates than the major telephone companies they thrived; when competition caused long-distance rates to plummet these companies collapsed.

Can the company compete in the marketplace of the real world? Quite often MLMs and other home-based opportunities try to compete with each other rather than making any serious attempt to gain market share from major manufacturers. Examine who the company is really trying to compete with. Do they have an advantage that will allow them to take market share away from companies that have established a dominant position in the marketplace and have probably existed far longer than the company you are thinking about joining?

What about timing? Is the market looking for the types of products the company is offering? Is the company in a position to take advantage of changes in the market? An example would be the trend to "go green." Consumer awareness of environmental concerns has probably never been higher. Companies offering products that capitalize on this have an advantage. The trend is so strong that many very large and long-established manufacturers have engaged in a practice known as "green washing." That is making their products appear to be "green" even though they may be nothing of the sort.

4- Consumer Value

This point is one so many people fail to consider. Perhaps they are wrapped up in the money angle or just haven't given it the proper thought. Simply put – does the product or service offer value to the consumer? While this ties in with competitive advantage, it is so much more than that. The economy is based on supply and demand, with the demand side being the key factor. If there is no demand the amount of supply does not matter. For the demand to exist the product must not only be something a consumer needs and wants, it has to have value to them as well. Value does not mean that something is cheap, it means that a consumer deems the product to be a worthwhile exchange for his or her cash. If it's not worth the money they won't buy it.

There is a very simple question that will determine if the company you are considering provides real value to the consumer. However, you must answer honestly. Question: If there was not a business opportunity attached would you still want to be a customer and buy the product or service the company offers? If the answer is "no" you should probably look elsewhere. If you wouldn't buy it why should anyone else? All too often people become involved with a company but stop when the business doesn't work out for them. When they quit they immediately stop using the product. That means the product had no real value other than the belief that they could make money. Had they determined that lack of value before getting involved they might not have wasted their time, energy, and cash. Conversely, if this is a product you absolutely want to have regardless of any business opportunity you may have found a winner if the other factors pass the test.

5- Reorder Rate

The typical reason for venturing into a home-based business opportunity is to create a secondary stream of income, often with the hope that it will grow large enough to become the primary source. In traditional businesses there are products that are big-ticket items with a high mark-up or profit per sale. This generally means low volume and often sporadic income. The other extreme is low profit but high volume item with sales that result in a steady income stream. This is where you will find most home-based businesses. The theory is that each customer will produce a small amount of profit but the volume will be high and the sales will be steady. The key to this model is repeat business.

There have been some MLM companies that sought out one-shot sales in products such as car alarms and water filters. The problem with those businesses is that as soon as you acquired a customer you had to go find another one because the initial one was not likely to need another water filter or car alarm any time in the near future. That is hardly the formula for building a steady stream of income.

To create that reliable income stream the product should be consumable. That means that the customer uses up, or consumes, the product and then needs to reorder it. It is those reorders that produce the residual income most people are seeking. It does not necessarily need to be a physical product for it to be considered consumable and any sort of monthly subscription payment could be considered a consumable product as well.

The key factor in building that reliable, residual income will be the reorder rate. How many customers who purchase products this month will purchase again the next month? What about the month after that? If the company has an extensive product line of items that their customers need and want it will make it much easier for those customers to reorder each month. Some companies have programs that provide discounts for those who commit to a monthly order while others may have an auto-ship program that automatically sends out products, such as vitamins, that ensures a consistently high reorder rate. The previous factor, consumer value, will play a large role here. If the consumer perceives that the products are valuable they will be more likely to reorder.

Finding out the reorder rate may not be easy. A company with a good one will probably be quick to tout it while those with a low rate would probably seek to hide it or camouflage it in some way. Be aware that many of the MLM companies have reorder rates that are very low, such as 10-20%. If 9 out of 10 customers are not ordering it can be very difficult to build a reliable, residual income.

6- Attrition

All businesses, no matter how exceptional, lose customers. It's going to happen so be prepared for it. What matters is how high the rate is, the lower the rate the easier it is to build a business. For a business to grow the customer base and order volume needs to increase. To grow the customer base new people have to join and shop, but before there can be growth the customers who left need to be replaced. In simple mathematical terms a company with one hundred customers and a 50% monthly attrition rate will need to attract fifty-one new customers to experience any growth at all the next month. A company with a 50% attrition rate is not one that is likely to be around very long. Many of the fad companies will experience rates that high or even greater after the initial boom has passed.

Inactive customers need to be factored into the attrition, many MLM companies will continue to list customers who haven't purchased in a very long time. When examining attrition look at how many customers actually ordered. If customers do not reorder are they really there?

So why do customers leave a company? It's simple, they leave when the reason for joining in the first place is no longer valid. This brings us back to value, where is the value for a customer? If the company does not offer a product or service with *real value* that people *really want* the attrition will most likely be high. So many people jump into opportunities without even considering this, they simply look at the fancy charts, graphs, pictures of fancy cars and think of all the money they expect to make. Their initial reason for joining was to make money, when that money doesn't materialize they quit.

Think objectively about why you would join the company you are considering. Is it only the money? If so you should think again. If the product doesn't offer enough of a reason for you to join, why would anyone else? Conversely, if people want the products without consideration of earning an income you may have found a very solid opportunity.

7- Cost of Entry

How much does it cost to get started? There may be an enrollment or membership fee as well as a product order. In the past many of the MLM companies could cost thousands of dollars to join if you wanted to build a business. If you would be selling product retail there was be inventory involved and you needed to purchase it up front. This was a process known as "front-loading" and a frequent trap of the MLMs and led to the phrase "garage qualified" – that was a tongue-in-cheek reference to the fact that you had so much product stored in your garage that you could no longer use it to park your car. Years later many distributors still have inventory that was never sold.

If you are starting a new venture you should do it the right way. What do you need to purchase to give yourself the greatest chance of success? You need to have product knowledge if you are going to intelligently communicate the benefits of the company to others. What do you need to buy to acquire that knowledge? Many companies will offer suggested starter packs at a discount when you first join. Cutting corners here could hurt you in the long run. You may also need to purchase a number of sales aids and other materials as well as attending training seminars or annual conventions. How much does all of this cost? Be aware that some of the companies treat their marketing executives as another profit center rather than as business partners. If the training material or events seem to be unreasonably priced then you should consider that a red flag and think very carefully about whether you want to sign with them.

Any type of business, whether traditional or home-based, is going to require some sort of investment. That investment is your cost of entry. Is it an amount that you can afford and are comfortable with? Can you afford to lose it if you determine that the business isn't right for you? If not perhaps you should be considering something else. One caveat – if you need to max out your credit card to join it probably is not the right opportunity for you.

8- Monthly Purchase Requirements

This is a big factor in how much attrition a company experiences. Is the monthly purchase requirement reasonable or are you required to purchase more than you really need? Are you purchasing things you would not ordinarily buy? Is it a product or service that you've never used before and are only buying because you have to in order be in the business? Are you required to buy product that you are supposed to resell to retail customers?

Many of the juice companies required distributors to purchase a case of product each month. This was significantly more than they could ever use themselves but the expectation was that they would resell it. Of course, many of them didn't and wound up with cases of product in their basements, garages, and storerooms.

Those cases are a stark reminder that the business is not working for them and they eventually quit. The juice companies are just one example, similar things happen with many other businesses. This is especially true of opportunities that tout just one product or only a handful of them. If you are considering this type of company can you realistically expect to move enough product so that you won't become a mini warehouse?

Ideally the purchase requirement would be a simple matter of switching brands. Customers who aren't spending additional money are much more likely to stay, especially if they like the products. If it is a purchase of something that wasn't used previously the price should be reasonable. If you find that the monthly purchases are a burden or are simply being added to credit card debt that is a warning sign and probably means this is not the right company for you.

9- Compensation Plan

Unfortunately this is the first thing many people look at when it should really be the last. If the business didn't pass muster with the first eight factors how much you are compensated is not going to matter. There isn't a pay plan in existence that can compensate for a poor product line or a bad business model. If there are no customers buying product what will you get paid on? Yet it is the compensation plan and the fantasy of a huge income that is the sizzle that sells people. Companies know this and often skew their compensation plans to put a lot of money in the hands of a very few people who can then flash big checks and push the fantasy of an extravagant lifestyle. It would easy if it were as simple as sell "x" get paid "y" but it's not. Compensation plans tend to be convoluted with many twists and turns with the bad points carefully camouflaged. One fact that you can take to the bank – there is no such thing as a perfect pay plan.

Simple math dictates that there is a finite amount of money available for compensation. If you see a plan that claims that it "pays to infinity" you can be certain that the money is being taken from somewhere or the company would be out of business in short order. A pay structure can tell you a lot about a company and what they expect because they will reward the activities that are important to them.

Ideally a compensation plan would be fair and balanced. It should reward people who are productive and help the company grow. However, many people have the idea that they should just sign up a few customers then sit back while other people do all the work. If everyone is waiting for someone else to build a business you can be fairly certain it will never happen. Companies create compensation plans to entice people to do the things that helps the company prosper. Successful companies are not just those that create a great product, they also reward their people for doing the right activities.

Many compensation plans are loaded with gimmicks that tend to be difficult to understand. There are terms like binary, stair-step, breakaway, unilevel matrix, and more. Some plans are deliberately confusing while others are fairly straightforward. You should have a copy of the compensation plan before you sign up. As stated earlier, no plan is perfect. There will be tradeoffs in them and you need to determine what is important for you.

Look at what you are compensated for. Are you paid for signing up customers, only on their purchases, or some combination? Are you paid on all purchases by your customers? That may seem obvious but it isn't necessarily the case. Do you receive more on personal customers as opposed to those who are introduced into your business by others? Do you receive bonuses or a higher rate of pay for advancing to a higher status? Are there bonuses for growth of your organization? Do you get paid for mentoring others? Many companies will pay for a car if you reach a certain status level, at what point does that happen?

Watch for takeaways. It's normal to be charged back for customer returns. Is money taken away for any other reason? Is there a quota that you have to meet each month or quarter? What happens if you don't reach it? Other than not meeting a personal purchase requirement, is there any other reason for not receiving a check? What happens to your business if you decide to stop working but continue to meet your purchase obligations?

How stable is the compensation plan? Has it been in place for a long time or is it constantly being changed? When a company alters a compensation plan they usually describe it as an enhancement and imply that pay is being increased, but is it? Or is it just being reshuffled? A company that constantly changes the pay plan is a cause for concern as it may indicate that the company is in financial trouble. If a plan is changing frequently can you count on the amount of money you'll be paid?

While there is no perfect compensation plan, some are better than others. Different plans appeal to different people. A plan that is an excellent choice for your friend may be a poor selection for you. This is an area where you have to do your homework. A note of caution, don't become paralyzed by your analysis. You probably won't figure it out completely until you experience it first-hand. Compensation plans also tend to evolve as the company changes and a plan could be better or worse down the road. Everything is a compromise and you simply need to make the best possible choice for you based on currently available information.

10- Risk

It would be nice if you could evaluate risk first in order to eliminate those opportunities that don't fall within the parameters of your tolerance for risk but it isn't that easy. Risk is determined by the answers you find when examining all of the other factors. Some people are comfortable with some level of risk while others refuse to accept any at all. Most people equate risk with the amount of money invested in a venture. To be sure, that is part of the risk equation but it is not all. So what are the different kinds of risk involved?

Money is the most obvious. How much is your initial investment? What is your ongoing financial commitment? Is any or all of that guaranteed or refundable? If not, can you afford to lose it? When entrepreneurs start a new business venture they often risk tens of thousands of dollars, in many cases their entire life savings. Your risk will not be anywhere near that but that doesn't mean you have to do it. If you are not comfortable with the level of financial risk then you should walk away.

For many a loss bigger than the money involved is the time spent. Can you afford the time away from your family, friends and other commitments? Investing this time could certainly make a major difference in your life if the business succeeds but that time is wasted if it doesn't. Are you willing to invest the time that is necessary?

Closing Thoughts

The evaluation factors can be a very useful tool when it comes to identifying a positive opportunity or eliminating a bad one. Remember though, even if you do find a company that seems to excel in every area that doesn't guarantee anything. Success or failure is most often the result of the effort and action of the individual pursuing the opportunity. A thorough evaluation can help level the playing field so that you have a fair chance of success.

When performing your analysis never forget that the person most likely to lie to you is *you*. Be as honest and objective as possible when looking at an opportunity, take off the blinders and throw away the rose-colored glasses. If you do your homework you may come up with an opportunity that is just right for you.

Richard J. Warren

Chapter Seven

Marketing Your Business

Chasing family and pestering friends is not generally a viable way of building a sustainable business of any kind. In my more than twenty years of working a home business I've never operated in that manner. So why is almost everyone who embarks on a network marketing business told to do just that? One reason is that the enroller wants their new builder to start quickly so they don't lose interest. Another reason is that friends and family are the low-hanging fruit that everyone has access to. Most people could easily list a hundred or more names on an initial contact list. Though people often say they don't know that many people, they could create a large list if they were properly guided.

Imagine if someone was told they could earn money for each name they list. They would receive $10 for each person they knew who also knew them well, $5 for each person they knew even if that person didn't know them very well, and $1 for anyone they knew of and had the ability to make contact with even if that person did not know them at all. How long do you think it would take them to earn $1,000? Probably only a matter of minutes and certainly less than an hour. All of us know a lot of people whether we realize it or not.

If we all know so many people why isn't that a good way of doing business? Several reasons. First, even a large list will be depleted fairly quickly. No matter how outstanding the products or the opportunity may be a lot of people will say "no" because they don't feel it's right for them. A lot of those negative responses will occur simply because someone is new to the business and doesn't understand how to properly communicate what they have. Another reason is that it is very discouraging to a new marketing executive when someone they are close to doesn't see their new business the same way they do. Being discouraged at the very start causes many people to quit.

The biggest reason for not immediately chasing friends and family is that you run a very high risk of being viewed as "one of those people" and have friends and family avoiding you. We have very likely come across people operating like that and they are generally treated like a pariah by those around them. To be clear, friends and family are not off limits, you just want them to come to you. If you do things the right way they will. So don't chase them. What often happens to those who rely on those closest to them is that they are out of business as soon as they run out of people on their friends and family list. Most don't have any kind of sales or marketing background and don't know how to find potential customers.

How do you get people to come to you? By being subtle and creating curiosity. If you are in the park feeding the pigeons do you run at them full speed while throwing food at them as hard as you can? Of course not, yet that's how many people approach friends and family. When they see any tiny opening they start vomiting up a long-winded, canned sales pitch oblivious to the fact that their prospect is rolling their eyes and searching for a means of immediate escape. The proper way of feeding pigeons is to unobtrusively drop bits of food while backing away slowly. The birds will peck at the food while following you in whatever direction you want to go. You acquire customers the same way. Provide your prospects with small bits of information, which creates curiosity, and you'll soon have them asking for more.

So if you don't approach friends and family right away how do you build a business? Like any business should, by building your brand in a way that allows for long-term, sustainable results. This will contradict what many will tell you but understand that their motivation most likely stems from their goals, not yours. The strategy of immediately going after everyone you know is great for them and would probably generate some short-term cash for you, but that doesn't lay a proper foundation for long term success. There are many other ways to market yourself and you need to do what best suits you and your personality. I will share the strategies that have worked well for me over the past two decades.

Establish Your Brand

When you join a company you have the option of hitching yourself to their brand and that is what most people opt to do. There are many advantages to doing so. You use their name recognition if it's an established company and can easily take advantage of company-branded marketing materials. This means that you can avoid many of the challenges of being new in business and allows you to take advantage of the company's reputation. Of course that assumes the reputation is a good one, but if it wasn't why would you have gone with them?

Another option is to establish and develop your own brand which has advantages and drawbacks of its own. This is what I have done. My own brand allows me to bring different, but related, things that I do under one umbrella. Mind you, I make no secret of the company I am affiliated with but it is a part of my overall brand. How this works with other things I do will become clear later in this chapter. A disadvantage is that you may need to create your own marketing material rather than use the company's. A clear advantage for someone starting out is that your own brand can camouflage a mistake. Even though you do a proper evaluation and select a company you think is right you may still come to realize it was not right for you. If you have your own brand you can select a different company without having to recreate everything and people may not perceive that you are jumping from one opportunity to another. If you use the company's brand it will be obvious to anyone who is paying attention.

Website

The website you use will depend on the business you are in and how you are branding yourself. In the past I used multiple sites. The primary one was branded as a consumer awareness site and made no mention of any company. That dovetailed with things I was doing as a consumer advocate. The site featured consumer oriented articles that provided information that related to my business. The idea was to have people request information or attend a webcast. I also used a website related to building a home business which was marketed differently. Another website was geared to those who are working the business with me. If you are using the company brand you will most likely use their website or one provided by them. In any case the purpose of much of your marketing will probably be to drive traffic to your website so this is not a place where you should be cutting corners.

Networking

In the context being used here, networking is meeting with other business people to share contacts and information in order to help each grow their business. Networking can occur in formal and informal settings and in groups large and small as well as one-on-one. I have used networking as a business building tool in several different sales oriented businesses for more than twenty-five years. It best suits my personality and if I could only use one strategy to build my business this would be it. However, it's not for everyone. To be a good networker you must take a genuine interest in other people's businesses or they will not help you with yours. There is an adage in networking that states, "givers gain." The meaning is that those who give to others without looking for reciprocation will find themselves on the receiving end quite often. When you help someone by giving them a business lead word gets around that you are a "giver" and people look to help you.

Networking takes several forms. There are formally structured groups large and small. Some are large organizations such as the Chamber of Commerce, local community organizations, for-profit networking businesses such as *LeTip, Business Networking International* (BNI), *National Association of Women Business Owners* (NAWBO), and many others. These groups often have a fee to join and monthly dues and required attendance at meetings. The meetings may be held weekly, biweekly or monthly at various times of the day. There is also an expectation that you will make referrals to other members on a fairly regular basis. There is certainly a commitment needed on your part but if you can develop a talent for networking it is well worth the effort. If you choose this to take this path in your business be sure to remember that the goal is to build relationships not make an immediate sale.

There are plenty of less formal networking opportunities as well that may be available at little or no cost. Many of the large organizations will have "mixers" that are open to members and non-members alike. There may be opportunities at social organizations and churches that host events that allow you to meet people.

To obtain the greatest benefit from networking you should have one-on-one "getting to know you" meetings with people you meet at the more formal events. This can be done of breakfast, lunch or coffee. The purpose is to get to know the other person and let them get to know you. It should not be viewed as an opportunity for you to make a sales pitch about your opportunity so keep it casual and low-key. After they find out what you do they may express an interest without you have to push it on them. If they aren't interested themselves they may be able to refer you to people who are. You should also be paying close attention to what they do and make a real effort to send potential customers to their business. Those referrals are the essence of networking.

Elevator Speech

An elevator speech is something that sums up what you do in thirty seconds or less. It is called an elevator speech because if you were talking to someone you just met on an elevator you would only have a very brief time for conversation. These speeches need to be short because people will not pay attention to you for much longer than that. In those thirty seconds they will size you up and make a decision about your knowledge and credibility. Those initial impressions are very hard to alter so you need to make those precious seconds count.

These speeches can be used anywhere but they are essential at networking events where you generally have thirty seconds to one minute to introduce yourself depending on the meeting format. You should have several versions of the speech depending upon your audience. Are you talking to potential customers? Business builders? Networking associates? Though the message should be similar each version would be different.

This is an example of the elevator speech I use at a networking meeting:

I work with a cutting-edge manufacturing company [may or may not use name]. We are successfully competing for market share in the consumer products industry with companies such as Proctor & Gamble, Lever Brothers, Colgate Palmolive, and Johnson & Johnson. We have a different business model that allows us to provide a superior, scientifically developed, and eco-friendly product line to consumers at prices that are highly competitive. My role is to educate consumers on the value of our brand.

The message is to the point and sounds very business-like. There is nothing about any business opportunity or any wording that would lead people to think of it as "one of those things." The words we use say a lot about who we are, so choose them carefully.

Social Media

In most businesses a social media presence is almost mandatory. If used wisely social media can greatly enhance your business. If it is used as a constant sales pitch you will be ignored. With so many social media platforms available you need to pick and choose the ones with the most appeal to the demographic of your target market. If you have a good knowledge of social media you can probably set it up yourself. If you are pressed for time or not really sure how to go about it you can do what I did and utilize the services of a social media consultant. For me it was well worth it.

I utilized Facebook, Twitter and LinkedIn. Using my brand and mimicking my website, I had accounts created for Facebook and Twitter. For LinkedIn I used my business profile since it is a business oriented platform. The key to using these sites effectively is to build a following and provide regular and updated content. You need to provide people with a reason to follow you. Remember, they won't be coming to see constant sales pitches.

Newsletters

Each month I sent out a consumer oriented newsletter. It linked back to my website and highlights a number of issues that would be of interest to most people. The newsletter was sent to those who are already customers, people I knew and have spoken to as well as many people I have never met who subscribed through my website or other social media. The goal of the newsletter was to add as many subscribers as possible. From this subscriber base I looked to have people request information about being a customer or attending a webcast. Everything was very generic and consumer oriented and there was no mention of any business opportunity in the newsletter. In my business 90% of the people who join do so to be customers so that is what I look to attract. This desire for the products is what makes the business so stable. From that customer base business builders will emerge naturally.

Blogging

This was a key part of my marketing strategy. It tied in my activities as a consumer advocate, the monthly consumer column I wrote for a small, local newspaper, one of my books (*Scammers, Schemers, and Dreamers*), and my network marketing business. There was a blog attached to my website with a new post each week. The posts went to my blog followers and were automatically distributed to my social media sites. A link to the latest blog entries was included on each monthly newsletter. In addition to writing my own articles I invited guest bloggers with expertise in areas related to my business to contribute. Most are eager to do so because it is added exposure for them and their business. I only invite those who would not be considered competition in any way.

The advantage of guest bloggers is that they will distribute their articles over their own social media which greatly increased my exposure.

Advertising & Leads

The advantages of today's technology provide a plethora of options and you should take advantage of as many as you can. Not so long ago your choices were much more limited. You could advertise for customers or buy leads. You can still do those things but today you can do even more as the internet evolves.

In addition to traditional print advertising in newspapers or other publications, it is easy to place ads on the internet that are targeted to your marketing demographic. There are plenty of places to place ads that are free and other places where you can do so at a nominal cost. With pay-per-click advertising programs you pay a certain amount every time someone views an ad; if they don't click you don't pay. Many sites, and search engines such as Google and Bing have advertising programs that allow you to set a daily ad budget. When the budgeted amount is reached the ads stop running for that day. You have the ability to adjust the budgeted amount at any time and to pause the ads when you don't want them to run. The advantage is that there are no surprises in terms of cost.

Buying leads is an option but it can get very expensive. This is a case where you will get what you pay for – hopefully. The cheapest leads you can buy are generally worthless. They've usually been sold to others before you and the odds of getting anything of value are fairly slim. The best leads are those which are new and you are the first or only person receiving them. They are also quite costly. Leads are generated by companies that place generic ads targeted at people looking to work from home. Even though the lead may be "fresh" there is no guarantee that the person is interested in what you have. My feeling is that it is better to generate your own leads through your marketing efforts rather than rely on a lead generating company.

How can you generate leads? Use the techniques mentioned earlier: networking, blogging, social media, newsletters, and pay-per-click advertising. Ads can be placed just about anywhere. The key is to place ads in places that are viewed by the people you are trying to attract. The ads should be constructed to appeal to your target demographic. What do they want? When using an internet ad you insert a hotlink that leads directly to your website. Once there they can fill out a form to request information or perhaps email or call depending on how you do business.

Summary

You can do everything right when you select a business. But even if the business is the best one on the planet and absolutely perfect for you, it will do nothing if you don't market it properly. When I joined my company more than twenty years ago I had the opportunity to talk to the top producer at the time. He said, "There were two keys to being successful. One – make appointments. Two – go on them. Everything else will take care of itself." To make appointments you need people to see. If you don't market your business you will have no on to see.

Chapter Eight

Starting the Right Way

If you've managed to find a company or opportunity that appeals to you what comes next? There may be a sense of urgency to jump right in with both feet, so step one is to simply "take a deep breath." If you've been approached by someone they'll want to get you signed up, on board, and working right from the outset. That is exactly what you should not do. If you've taken the time to carefully evaluate what was available and located something that seems to suit you and your needs you don't want to blow it now. That doesn't mean you should spend a great deal of time planning what you are going to do, but you should be properly prepared and begin your business with a concrete plan instead of blindly diving in the moment you sign on the dotted line.

How you start is often a critical factor in the ultimate success or failure of your business. How long has your enroller been working the business? Are they new? Have they been successful? If they are new that isn't a deal breaker by any means but you do need to dig a little deeper. What you are looking for is a support team, who are the people your friend or relative is working with? Are they successful? If they aren't it doesn't mean you can't be; it just means that you may not be able to rely on them for support. Would you be able to proceed under those circumstances?

Once you've decided who you are going to sign with the next step is to take another deep breath. Before making a commitment find out from your support team what they believe next step is. If you hear the nonsense about making a list of everyone you know and calling them immediately you might want to reconsider signing, unless calling that list is what *you* want to do. Remember this is *your* business, not theirs. If you do receive an answer you're comfortable with then by all means sign. Just don't immediately start pitching something you don't know that much about. So what *should* you do next?

Use the Product or Service.

No matter how you want to spin it you are selling a commodity of some kind. To do so properly you have to be familiar with whatever it is. How can you sell something if you haven't used it yourself? If it's a service sign up for it, if it's a product line try it – all of it. Product oriented companies typically offer a discounted package of some sort to their new customers. Purchase the largest one available (within reason). In an effort to save money people will often join a company but only place a minimum size product order that is not representative of what the company offers. That is not a good way to start. If you are going to make a commitment to work a business that commitment includes buying and using the products. If you can't afford to do so then this is probably not a good opportunity for you and you should consider doing something else.

Set Specific Goals.

Why are you venturing into a home-based business? What do you hope to achieve. When do you hope to achieve it? Goals need to be SMART:

Specific – what exactly do you want? Do not be vague.

Meaningful – what does your goal mean to *you*?

Attainable – is it something that is really possible to achieve?

Realistic – is it realistic in terms of your present circumstances?

Trackable – Can your progress be measured? Goals should be written down. The very act of putting pen to paper solidifies them in your mind. The most important aspect of your goal is the date by which you want to achieve it. A goal without a deadline is merely a wish and wishful thinking rarely gets you what you want.

Create a Plan

Like any legitimate business you need a business plan that will lead you to the achievement your goals. What are you going to do? How are you going to do it?

When will you do it; what are your store hours? What resources do you need? What help do you need? From whom? This does not need to be some formal document with charts and graphs; a simple, one-page plan can work just fine as long as it provides the necessary details. The idea is to outline what you are going to do and then, this is the important part – go do it.

Form a Team

Initially your team may be just you, or you and your spouse. Quite often you will team up with the person who introduced you to the company or their immediate support team. You should also be teaming up with people you introduce to the business. Working a business is much easier, and a lot more fun, if it is more than just you. A group of people working toward a common goal has the ability to share energy and resources and make it more rewarding for all of those involved.

A team also includes people who aren't in your business. These people may include a website provider, social media consultant, advertising specialist, etc. An accountant may also be in the mix since this is a business and you should be doing tax planning to take advantage of all the allowable deductions for the business expenses you are sure to accumulate.

Business Tools

Professionally produced business cards are a must unless you are working exclusively online. They are often the first impression people will have of you. Do you want to hand them something you printed off of your computer at home? If you are using the company brand you can probably purchase cards through them. If you are creating your own brand you should still be able to acquire high quality business cards at a reasonable cost. If you want to be treated like a professional you need to act like one. That includes how you present yourself in terms of dress. That doesn't mean you need to wear a suit and tie, but you should dress in a way that projects the image you striving for.

Depending on your business you may need a website. Some companies provide one and others have approved vendors who offer sites that meet the internet guidelines of the company. Some sort of web presence is essential in today's business climate, how sophisticated it needs to be depends on the type of business.

Training Material

Companies will offer training material to help you build your business. Some of it may be free or have a nominal cost. It should be noted that some companies use training material as a profit center and encourage you to buy as much as possible. A major red flag is if the person who introduced you to the business earns a commission on your purchases of training material which may entice them to push more than you really need. Some of the MLM company representatives could make more on training material than the actual sale of products. That kind of company is not one you should be involved with.

There is plenty of material available from outside vendors. You can find books, audio, and video to help with sales, marketing and other aspects of building a business.

Books

Books can be a low-cost way of acquiring knowledge in areas where you are lacking. There are plenty of good books on business networking, sales, marketing and much more.

The following are five titles I recommend:

7 Habits of Highly Effective People - Stephen Covey

Good to Great - Jim Collins

Positioning: The Battle for Your Mind - Al Ries & Jack Trout

The Power of Focus - Jack Canfield, Mark Victor Hanson, and Lee Hewitt

The Tipping Point - Malcolm Gladwell

Chapter Nine

Avoiding Traps

In any business there are roadblocks and traps that can snare you along the way. Most are stealthy and slip in without you realizing they are there. The business that has been humming along nicely suddenly hits a wall and you don't understand why. This should not be confused with the flat spots that happen naturally. No business, no matter how well it is run, will ever move on a constant upward trajectory. Whether seasonal variations or just a pause for some unexplained reason, flat spots will come and go and you just need to work through them. A trap is something different.

Traps are something you fall into because you weren't paying proper attention or changed something in the way you do business. They also happen because you allowed your focus to be shifted away from what is important. There are a number of traps large and small, we will examine the most common ones and look at ways to avoid them.

Management Mode

This is one that seems to happen to every new person. You get started the right way and begin enrolling customers. Your business starts growing and you find one or more individuals who also want to build a business. You help them get started and coach them along, as you should. The new builders start enrolling customers and the business grows nicely. Then it happens. You start focusing on what you builders are doing. You set up trainings and presentations, you handle follow up, you make sure your people are up to date on promotions and incentives, you solve problems and put out fires and do everything else necessary to manage your business. Then you get a business report and wonder what went wrong and why your business isn't advancing as expected. For the answer look in the mirror.

What happened was that you fell into management mode and stopped doing the activities that got you there in the first place, you focused more on management than marketing. As your business grows it certainly is necessary to manage things but you need to do that *in addition to* the marketing to bring in new customers.

Energy Suckers

We all know those people who are so needy that they seem to suck every ounce of energy out of you. They will certainly appear in your business. They contact you for every little thing even though they could easily find what they needed if they exerted a minimal amount of effort. You will have people that want you to do everything for them and want constant training and support. Some of these things are necessary and expected, the important thing is to know where to draw the line.

It is essential to help people as much as possible and be supportive but it should not be a burden. If you have someone who is constantly asking for information don't just give it to them, show them how to find it for themselves. Initially you will probably be doing presentations for them. When you do make sure they are there and get them to participate. That should help them develop the confidence to do presentations on their own.

Sometimes you have an energy sucker that is an incredible burden yet they add nothing to the business. They don't bring in any new customers and probably never will. When this happens you should wish them well but tell them you don't have the time to help them. You may even suggest that this is not the business for them and they should pursue a different type of venture. By doing so you are doing them, and you, a great favor.

Pushing Ropes

A common lament is, "if only I could motivate my team." You can't, so don't even try. Motivation comes from within. You support them, encourage them and celebrate their successes large and small. But you can't motivate them. It can be frustrating because *you* see how much they need it but they either don't see it or, more likely, they just don't care. Trying to drag an unmotivated person along is like pushing a rope.

Inevitably you will enroll people with great ability and others with a great need who could really be helped by your business. They come on board and say all the right things and you're sure you have a winner. You do everything properly on your end and wait for them to take off. And you wait, and wait but nothing happens. It is extremely frustrating because you know how good they could be if only they were as motivated as you.

Experience will teach you that you can't trust what people say. They probably aren't lying and mean it at the time they say it. But when it's time to act they don't. They don't want it bad enough, they aren't hungry. You need to learn not to believe the words, only the actions. People who are serious will not only tell you, they'll show you. So stop pushing the rope and move on.

Coasting

Despite what you've probably been told or may have read, it takes a very, very long time for a business to grow to a point of critical mass where it is self-sustaining. There will always be attrition and it's rare for a business to bring in enough new customers to cover that attrition all by itself. A typical pay structure or matrix generally pays to a certain depth and growth that occurs below that point does not impact your business. As a business matures the customers are coming in at deeper and deeper levels.

Perhaps at some point in time you've reached your goals and are bringing in the money you desire and don't want to work as hard. That's perfectly acceptable. However, if you don't want attrition to whittle away at your business you need to shift from growth mode to maintenance mode. Just don't ignore it completely. If you are maintaining you business you still need to do follow up, handle problems, stay in touch with business builders and do some marketing. Think of it more as keeping your customers happy. You should do some of your marketing such as newsletters and blogs and maintain your web and social media presence. You may even be able to delegate it to some of your people in exchange for letting them have whatever leads may come in. Hopefully you will still bring in some customers here and there. Whatever you do don't simply walk away unless you are prepared to give it up completely.

Enrolling People the Wrong Way

This trap was saved for last because it is probably the biggest one and easiest to fall into. When someone is looking to join your business and build one of their own there are things they need to do to have the greatest chance of success. This varies from business to business but usually involves purchasing enough of the product to develop a good knowledge of it. They may also need some essential tools for building that business. People who do all of those things are coming in the right way. Unfortunately not everyone does so.

For a variety of reasons some people will try to avoid coming in the right way. The reason is often financial, they simply don't have the money to do it properly even though the cost isn't that high. Perhaps they like to do things their own way and don't want to listen, perhaps there's some other reason. Whatever the reason the solution is the same – don't bring them into your business. That may seem harsh or you may really,

really need to bring someone in. You'll certainly be tempted to do so, especially early on when your business isn't that big. I was that way in the beginning but often regretted it when I did. I wasted a lot of time and energy needlessly until I figured out that it wasn't worth it. The situation was reminiscent of an experience I had when I was new to sales.

Many years ago I was a new and struggling insurance agent I was on a sales call when I learned a powerful lesson. I was given a lead that had a high probability of closing and I needed to make a sale to hit my quota for the month. I went to see a couple that was ten or so years older than I was with the insurance being for him. I was, and still am, a proponent of needs-based selling where you determine what the prospect needs or wants and present them with their options. I did just that in this case providing a solution that met their stated needs. It did not go smoothly. The husband was very abrasive, challenging everything I said. The wife was telling him to go ahead with the purchase and the sale was pretty much assured but he wouldn't let up. It was really getting to me. After I explained one of the things he was making a big deal about he essentially implied I was a liar and overtly stated I didn't know what I was talking about. At that point I had had enough. I closed my book, stood up, and told him he should find another insurance agent because I couldn't work with him. They were stunned when I walked out and as I was getting into my car I could hear them screaming at each other. I could only imagine how excruciating it would have been to have that man as a client. Not having that sale meant I didn't make quota that month and didn't receive my monthly draw. Even though walking away hurt me financially I felt so empowered by doing so and never hesitated to walk away from a bad deal again.

That lesson carried over into my network marketing business. Early on I did bring people the wrong way because I didn't understand the implications of doing so. Once I figured that out I stopped. Understand that I will allow anyone to come in as a customer and those customer enrollments are the lion share of my business. It's when someone wants to partner with me in the business that I draw the line. Make no mistake, they are a partner when they come in as a business builder and I treat them as such. If they want to be my partner they must come in the right way or I won't work with them. If they insist on coming in the wrong way they can do so but the amount of time and energy I commit to them will be minimal.

Summary

There are many, many traps and bad habits we fall into in whatever we do. The ones listed above are the more common situations but they are not the only ones. Be aware of them and whenever your business seems to take a wrong turn step back and see if you've fallen into any bad habits. Keep your goals in mind and always keep moving toward them. You may find that you are more susceptible to certain traps so you must always keep your guard up.

Chapter Ten

Conclusion

You've gotten this far and hopefully you have a better understanding of the good and bad of home business opportunities. There are no guarantees but if you follow the evaluation steps in an honest manner you should get a pretty good idea of whether an opportunity has merit. Keep in mind that most are highly flawed and you will have to sift through a lot of garbage to find one that might actually work for you.

The type of business you choose depends a lot on you and your personality. What do you like to do? Do you like talking to a group of people and demonstrating products with the idea of making sales on the spot? If so, a party-plan type of company that sells products retail may be for you. Do you like managing and working with a team? That's a different type of business. Are you a stay-at-home mom that wants to work with others like you? Someone who wants to work exclusively on line? Someone who wants to market a service rather that products? There are businesses that appeal to each of those situations. That's why there is no business that is right for everyone and you need to do some digging to find one that's right for you.

The best advice I can leave you with is to ignore the internet hype, don't listen to those pushing the fad du jour, and ignore the books and articles pushing can't-miss systems of building a massive network marketing business. As hard as it may be to do, don't jump into a business because your best friend or relative is doing it. Think of all that noise as nothing more than the voices of shills in a three-card Monte game.

If you truly do want to build a network marketing business choose to partner with a company that meets all of the evaluation criteria. Missing even one reduces your chance of success, missing more just increases your risk exponentially. There is one thing to do before starting your evaluation that is absolutely imperative – take the blinders off!

Good Luck!

Richard J. Warren

About the Author

Richard J. Warren

After a career as a Certified Financial Planner, Richard Warren moved to Las Vegas from Long Island, New York in 2003. He is an author and freelance journalist and was the Consumer Columnist for *The Vegas Voice* newspaper until moving to North Carolina in 2016. His book *Scammers, Schemers, and Dreamers*, was released in June 2014. Co-written with Elisabeth Daniels, the former head of the *Nevada Fight Fraud Task Force*, the book explores the human toll of being victimized by fraud.

A seasoned real estate investor, he is the author of *A Rehabber's Tale: The Reality of Fixing and Flipping Real Estate*. Richard has written more than 150 articles related to real estate investing. In addition his fiction was recently featured in *Tales from the Silver State*, an anthology of Emerging Nevada Writers.

Richard@richkat.us

Richard J. Warren